Eleven Rooms

Claire Dyer holds a BA in English & History from the University of Birmingham and an MA in Victorian Literature & Culture from the University of Reading. She is currently studying for an MA in Poetry at Royal Holloway, University of London. She lives in Reading, Berkshire. *Eleven Rooms* is her first collection.

Two Rivers Press First Collection Series
Kate Behrens, *The Beholder* (2012)
Claire Dyer, *Eleven Rooms* (2013)
Tom Phillips, *Recreation Ground* (2012)

The First Collection Series was launched in 2012 to provide an opportunity for emerging poets, already visible on the reading circuit or in pamphlet form, to have a debut, self-contained statement collaboratively shaped, edited, designed and published.

Also by Two Rivers Poets:
Paul Bavister, *Miletree* (1996)
Paul Bavister, *Glass* (1998)
Paul Bavister, *The Prawn Season* (2002)
Kate Behrens, *The Beholder* (2012)
Adrian Blamires, *The Effect of Coastal Processes* (2005)
Adrian Blamires, *The Pang Valley* (2010)
Joseph Butler, *Hearthstone* (2006)
Jane Draycott and Lesley Saunders, *Christina the Astonishing* (1998)
Jane Draycott, *Tideway* (2002)
John Froy, *Eggshell: A Decorator's Notes* (2007)
David Greenslade, *Zeus Amoeba* (2009)
A. F. Harrold, *Logic and the Heart* (2004)
A. F. Harrold, *Postcards from the Hedgehog* (2007)
A. F. Harrold, *Flood* (2009)
A. F. Harrold, *The Point of Inconvenience* (2013)
Ian House, *Cutting the Quick* (2005)
Gill Learner, *The Agister's Experiment* (2011)
Kate Noakes, *The Wall Menders* (2009)
Victoria Pugh, *Mrs Marvellous* (2008)
Peter Robinson, *English Nettles and Other Poems* (2010)
Peter Robinson (ed.), *Reading Poetry: An Anthology* (2011)
Peter Robinson (ed.), *A Mutual Friend: Poems for Charles Dickens* (2012)
Lesley Saunders, *Her Leafy Eye* (2009)
Lesley Saunders, *Cloud Camera* (2012)
Susan Utting, *Houses Without Walls* (2006)
Susan Utting, *Fair's Fair* (2012)

Eleven Rooms

Claire Dyer

For June,
with love,
Claire
12/6/13

TWO RIVERS PRESS

First published in the UK in 2013 by Two Rivers Press
7 Denmark Road, Reading RG1 5PA.
www.tworiverspress.com

© Claire Dyer 2013

The right of the poet to be identified as the author of the work has been asserted by him in accordance with the Copyright, Designs and Patents Act of 1988.

All rights reserved. No part of this publication may be reproduced, stored in or introduced into a retrieval system, or transmitted, in any form, or by any means (electronic, mechanical, photocopying, recording or otherwise) without the prior written permission of the publisher.

ISBN 978-1-901677-91-1

2 3 4 5 6 7 8 9

Two Rivers Press is represented in the UK by Inpress Ltd and distributed by Central Books.

Cover design by Nadja Guggi using Pete Hay's illustrations.
Text design by Nadja Guggi and typeset in Janson and Parisine.

Printed and bound in Great Britain by Imprint Digital, Exeter.

Dedication: Street-map

I am a camera-holding-god
with aspirations to reach the sun.
Below me, someone has quilted parks,
sewn a river, moulded

brick-built worlds next
to churches and ponds,
raised palaces, carved
a mania of motorways.

But all I see are the flattened
tops of things. I yearn
for texture and leaf-fall,
for pavements, for height.

I am a camera-holding-god,
shutter-click the town
where I was born, capture
roads knitted to patterns vaguely

known, print my mother
in the drive of number five
Acacia Road, have her look up,
                              scan the sky.

*Also for
my sister*

By the same author:

Fiction
The Moment, Quercus (2013)
The Perfect Affair, Quercus (2014)

Acknowledgements

My thanks to the editors of *South*, *The IMPpress*, *Other Poetry*, *Orbis*, *Domestic Cherry*, *Reading Poetry* (Two Rivers Press), *Feeding the Cat & other stories and poems* (Cinnamon Press), *The Lampeter Review*, *Antiphon*, *R. U. Taking the Biscuit?* (Reading Creative Arts Anthology 2009), *One Moment's Clouds* (Reading Creative Arts Anthology 2012), *BlueGate Poets' Anthology 2012*, *LiterARTure* and *Soul Feathers* (Indigo Dreams) in whose publications some of these poems, or versions of them, have appeared.

My thanks also go to the judges and organizers of the Owen Barfield Poetry Competition 2009, York Open Poetry Competition 2010/2011 and The Cinnamon Press Poetry Award 2011 for awarding prizes to 'Fisherman', 'Strada, Broad Street' and *Dowry* (pamphlet). 'Dowry (i)', 'Dowry (ii)' and 'Malta' were published in *Jericho & other stories and poems* (Cinnamon Press).

Contents

One Boy | 1
The Day Elvis Died | 2
In her Grandmother's Larder | 3
Triptych | 4
Cornish Wagon | 5
The Metamorphosis of Fish | 7
Elsie & Boy | 9
The Tree Harvesters | 10
French Lessons | 11
Visiting the Seals | 12
At Breakfast | 13
Levendale | 14
Cupboard Love | 15
The Collector | 16
Cinderella, Backwards | 17
A Man with Pale Grey Eyes | 18
Flying with Dragons | 19
At Blake's Lock | 20
Lovers' Vows | 21
Only Archaeology | 22
Plunder | 23
Eleven Rooms | 24
Ab Initio | 25
Dowry (i) | 26
Dowry (ii) | 27
Marriage, Backwards | 28
Wall Angels | 29
Escapology | 30
Fisherman | 31
Soundless | 32
Punctuation | 33
Reversal | 34
Talking to a Dead Horse | 35
Strada, Broad Street | 36
The Love Song of Nowhere Place | 37

Afterwards | 38
Mistranslations | 39
Grattage | 41
Cwm yr Adar | 42
Llantwit Sands | 43
Malta | 44
Cuffs | 45
Exhibition | 46
Photograph, 1959 | 47
Taking Tea at the Savoy | 48
It Sparks | 49
Cader Idris | 50
Afterword: Dearest | 51

One Boy

That summer was the first, the first I rode
the back of a motorbike behind a boy,
one who'd found a fleeting kind of fame

on *Blue Peter* for hatching duck eggs
in the kitchen of his father's farm.
The boy with a hole in his heart.

A field, rattle of hard earth under our wheels,
dust and swags of two-stroke, the sun slipping
behind trees and that inch of electric air,

my arms around his brittle waist,
the jumper his mother knitted, its hot wool,
one plain, one purl, one breath away.

At the gate he smiled at me.
No start, no end, it was just that,
one summer, one bike, one boy.

The Day Elvis Died

we were packing.
Already the moving vans
were a low rumble across the Severn

bringing with them the ending of our Wales,
the loss of our elderflower valley,
our precious skim of sea.

It had been a time of horses,
bottle-green school uniforms,
the boy in the coal shed, his hand

on my waist. It had been about cigarettes
and village shops, about Thursday
Youth Club and *Songs of Praise* filming

in the church. The summers had been
long and hot, winters blew in on the wind.
We'd tasted leeks, sweet after the first frost

and our house stood bright and white
above the lane to the beach.
It had been about wonderment

and what we didn't know about love:
about pocketfuls of rainbows
and crying in the chapel, suspicious

minds, and softly as I leave you,
about hearts of stone. We packed
away the radio just before the news.

Why, I asked, standing at her bedroom door,
is it wall-to-wall Elvis today?
Perhaps, my sister said, *it's his birthday.*

In her Grandmother's Larder

she is maestro, baton-taps an orchestra
of crockery, is gracious with sugar bowl and cake,
conjures afternoon tea for royalty. The door
is softly closed on air sharp with summer.
It listens to the chink and plash, the marble-run
of cherries, watches the kiss of apron hem
on slate, her garden feet; marvels at the lacework
of flour, small dust. And, at an altar of Pyrex
and tin, she marries a man with grey-green eyes,
weighs angels and demons on copper scales,
spoons the mix into fluted paper cases, bakes
at Gas Mark 5, leaves to cool for a while.

Triptych

In a house of corners and stairs
and my grandmother's cooking
is a room of permanence and wood,
with a too-small window and a bed that's a boat
built from soft history and wheat,
where I wait with my sister beside me
to be orphan, adventurer, queen –
where I wait with her to be old.

In a house of morning and birdsong
and my children grown away, grown from home,
I am smoothing the night from the sheets,
soothing the watchful, him wakeful, his touch
on my hip, his younger self's face as he sleeps.
Outside is Tuesday, the hour of click and stretch
and, if I listen hard with my head
on one side, I can hear a distant child cry.

In a house of salt wash and light
and my bed carried singing to the sea,
I cover the counterpane
with petals and pictures,
sleep with my skin to the sun
and the talking of trees,
feel the velvet speak of his breath in my hair –
wait to be orphan, adventurer, queen.

Cornish Wagon

Museum of English Rural Life, 2012

Seeing it stops my heart the length of a word.
I thought I'd forgotten
but, in its scarred wood, its wheels
shoulder-high and marked out

with hammer blows, his father's name
painted on a panel at the front,
is that moment after the harvest
when Joe said, *Whoa, Boy*,

and the horse stilled, the heat rising
sweet and thick from him. Mill Lane
and the Lower Field were evening,
the air above us weary, and birds

sang like needlecraft. They stitched
the sky, almost silk it was.
Not so our clothes, Joe's and mine,
rough with leftover grain.

It stuck to our skin as he kissed me,
his shirt dull with dust
and sweat from between
his shoulder blades.

We lay together when the clouds were dark
and him hard like stone.
His love afterwards
had no heat left, was what

remained, he said. It made me
remember water from the yard pump
when it has the sun in it.
And afterwards: a splinter

in my palm from the wagon-bed
that dug deep, hurt
in colour, and the child
who would bring me here

to this and you who, turning say,
Hey, let's go. So I leave,
one long look back from the door,
my hand still sore, still stinging.

The Metamorphosis of Fish

I have given birth to fish
and, after the last push,

watched scales become skin;
have pressed soft

the mania of veins
netting purple

near their butterfly hearts;
waited

as lilac arms stretched,
flailing from fins, as legs

split from mermen tails.
The kick of them still ghosts

the ghosts in my ribs.
There was always shipwreck

in the wake, debris in a
ferrous tide,

but I was held fast
by the wisdom,

by the grey-green
of their ocean eyes.

I have drunk the scent
of the sea deep

in the lozenge
of their limbs, been

revised from captain
to hostage, from goddess

to prey; know I have no might,
am no Amphitrite,

foretell there will be
exodus,

that these Triton-lords
will surge, will swim.

Elsie & Boy

He stands in the back room at Carroll Avenue.
Elsie's things are breathing darkly –
table, chairs, hearth, all heavy, and trees
are swallowing the window frame.

He asks the carpet to let him go
to motorways and all-night bars.

Elsie waits in the kitchen, hands
like prayers on the tabletop. She bends,
picks a button loose so her housecoat gapes,
lets the cake mix spoil, hears the front door

close on his borrowed case, clean socks
and vests, his best shirt – pressed.

The Tree Harvesters

We all got to sew –
the aunts, my sisters, our mother wearing green,
squatting near the river rocks, an unsteady sun
huge and low, the men not yet back.

We stitched the story of those
who harvested trees. The roots we tacked
in red, and birds plucking seeds
like fish bits from the wash of boats.

The cuts were sharp, we didn't want
to show how trees can tear,
suture in the sound of their felling.
We didn't want to show the dust,

the sinews in the women's arms,
so we made the ground clean,
their skin smooth, their clothes dazzle.
We hemmed in the crushed one,

but not her cries, nor why the men
stopped their ears with small hard hands.
We seamed the fable
of the seven women and the trees

they gathered as it had been passed to us
by all our mothers, of the temple they built
to honour the gods,
how it failed to appease them.

*After a mural at Reading International Solidarity Centre,
London Street, Reading.*

French Lessons

I started talking to the cats in French today,
because the silence in the house is astonishing.

Not like the gone-out-back-soon quiet of before
but something that's yellow and flat

and has no doors in it. And your keys
are gone from the shelf in the hall,

the fridge has begun to look baleful;
its shelves pulse vacancy. Of course it rained –

rain that said *I'm not going to stop
and, by the way, it's the end of summer*,

but I watched the road for a while
in case you walked up the drive

with the sun in your pocket.
It would be the size of an orange, and as bright.

So I say *Viens, Bonjour* and *Mon Dieu, il pleut!* to the cats.
They stare at me as I look into this silence

that's yellow and flat and has no doors in it.

Visiting the Seals

They'd stopped the boats to Skomer
so we walked to Wooltack Point.

The October sun and sky were low,
the sea sheet metal. A few walkers,

and Darwin was there.
In Deer Park we looked down.

Foam snagged the rocks. It deafened us.
Giants had taken bites, I traced

teeth marks in the cliffs.
On the edge I was already falling.

Then the seals. Fat white pups, slugs
waiting for the tide. Everywhere

fish, dark kelp, the hump sound of crying.
I couldn't see their eyes but I did.

They had me in them.
The guidebook said to speak softly.

We were in the car driving back
when the waves came.

At Breakfast

I tell her I don't remember the stairs,
the lift, its accordion doors,
how the light fell that morning,

if we dared one another to tread
the cracks that summoned dragons
and princes on black stallions

from beneath the marble floor.
I don't remember the room,
its curtains, lampshades, the shapes

made by its window frames,
the scent of sandalwood, pine.
But there we are, ladies in lavender,

aged seven and nine and it's theatre,
linen cloths, sugar tongs,
toast sliced thin.

We drank a swimming pool of tea
and Dad said how, just then,
we began to be the women we would become.

We still don't know if this was a wonder
or a grief, whether someone was watching
who, like him, remembered butter, rations,

when love was the colour blue.
A waiter hovers.
The hospital's close by.

Levendale

We watched the walls
square their shoulders
the day the wreckers came.

Glassless windows
held their breath
in the before-blow silence.

We could already see
bare brown earth,
flat with anonymity,

hiding behind hoardings
that read *Care Home for the Elderly*.
We knew the traffic,

saw, in a constant loop,
the filmings of our past:
deckchairs gathering

on the lawn, firewatchers shouting,
batter beaten in kitchen bowls,
silver cutlery gleaming,

blankets and warm toast,
stories under the covers,
the day our mother died.

We heard the hall clock chiming,
Nan's miniature roses stretching
and, when the house fell,

behind the roar came
brickdust, grainy on our lips.
We drew it in like food.

Cupboard Love

for Jared & Liam

Nan used it to keep her shoes in,
neat pairings in navy and cream
but, when she bequeathed it,
they'd long gone to the ploughed fields
where ghosts do their dancing
and we filled it with gleanings:
haphazard card-clusters from birthdays
and Valentines, curls of baby-blond hair,
drawings of the potato-shaped people
we used to be, notes the tooth fairy left,
exercise books and creatures in clay,
pictures of pets, programmes from plays
with you as *Third Shepherd* or *Tree*,
my grandfather's bible, a bag of old coins,
letters and clippings, a clock with no key.
You are long gone, with your bank books,
your passports, your dreams.
We remain here with this spilling of things
and doors that won't close.

The Collector

She gets them from thrift shops, markets,
and Aunt May's flat on the Cromwell Road.
Like orphans.

Denby, Derby, Doulton, Wedgwood –
single cups, odd plates,
a sugar bowl without its lid.

Her children.
Each day she adjusts her still life
in ways only she can see,

imagines before – a kitchen sink,
light caught in fists of bubbles,
a cup, a wife washing off lipstick marks

left by the woman next-door.
The chip is large enough
to run a finger over and feel

a roughness like teeth.
In the collector's studio
it is quiet. The fire fizzes

its electric coils at her feet,
rain quills against the window
and, at last, she picks up

her cutting tool, nips and clips
around the gilt until she has
enough to make a picture with.

She calls the work *Phoenix*.

Cinderella, Backwards

after John Glenday & Angela Carter

Happily Ever After he unbends his knee,
plucks a glass slipper from her perfect foot,
thinks, *Surely, this should be fur?*

Next, he uncurls his lip at the bloodied
stumps of some sisters' toes, mounts
a vast black stallion and rides away

as an invitation is unprinted,
a Ball unplanned, exquisite footwear
is never left upon a stair. And she goes back

to midnight to unchime the clock,
dance in reverse with a man who will one day
unsearch for her while six footmen

return to mice, a golden coach to pumpkin
as an orchestra untunes, her dress re-rags,
an impossible Fairy Godmother dissolves to dust.

And there will be a Prince somewhere
who unbelieves in love again as she sweeps
Once Upon A Time back in through the door.

A Man with Pale Grey Eyes

A pre-dawn Jubilee Line sign says
The last westbound train has gone.
So, she decides to climb

steel steps to Canada Square as wings begin
to crack her clothes, her skin. Their unfurling
hurts the silence, the dark. Dust, broken feathers,
    flakes of new-grown bone spin
to the ground as she shakes, shakes
    the pain of it.

She runs, runs, leaps to air, spirals to the tower tops,
to vapour trail hems of yesterday's planes,
turns westbound, beats to hover, sees the lights of London
    beckon her home.
But, here, here is where the gulls cry and she
    can smell the sea,

so flies east, over the brown estuary to the lifting sun,
watches Margate wake, hears Calais hum. Past Ostende,
past Den Haag, the North Sea winds fling her
    to the streets of Haarlem –
where she folds her wings back in, covers them with
    clothes, with skin,

where she asks a man with pale grey eyes to buy her beer
and feed her, where, when the westbound trains run again,
she decides to stay.

Flying with Dragons

Last night in my dream there were dragons.
A zinc sun smote the wild grasses,
the air was purple, filled with pollen and dust
and, at the end of land above a shifting
sea that breathed spume, breathed blue,
I heard them come.

Footsteps like heartbeats, they ran in formation behind me –
a squadron of heat, flame and bright burning eyes.

They lifted, a skein, were green and steel,
each wing-beat was language, myth,
pause and repeat. I clamoured to catch one,
feel his neck-flex, ride him out hard
to the thin curve of the earth. But they flew fast,
flew high, left me empty of sky,

left me nothing but red and the heft
of their hearts beating huge in the dark of their chests.

At Blake's Lock

I had forgotten the river,
its sound and its waterfall,
the green of it –

forgotten the launching
of birds, the heron's
plastic watchfulness,

its only movement an eye,
a feather-flick – forgotten
the reach of trees, their branch-dipping

offering, the tang of pillow-soft leaves –
forgotten the sun's marbling,
its quiet mirror-darts –

forgotten the scoop of oars,
glide and scull of boats,
how we closed our eyes,

white-blinded by the sky,
but could still see, how time
rested on a blade edge,

unblemished, light.
At Blake's Lock I remembered
these things, their rushing, you.

Lovers' Vows

April was soft from the window,
was bluebells, gillyflowers, Lady's Mantle
and how the birds sang. Was Sweet
William, sedum, anthemis tinctoria,
Leopard's Bane, the beech hedge –
its fretwork, and the smudge of aircraft
overhead. Was Cassandra's handkerchief,
two topaz crosses, silk winders, Lottery fish,
an ivory pounce box, a miser's purse
and lace collar, Jane's needlecase, dried
herbs, jelly moulds, the word – samphire.
Was remnants of hand-blocked wallpaper
and Lovers' Vows: A PLAY IN FIVE ACTS,
PERFORMED AT THE THEATRE ROYAL,
COVENT-GARDEN, FROM THE GERMAN
OF KOTZEBUE BY MRS INCHBALD, LONDON:
Printed for G. G. & J. Robinson, Paternoster-Row,
1798 [Price, Two Shillings]. Was preservation.

Only Archaeology

Caversham Court, 2011

With wand of swan feather and Black Mulberry wood
I conjure a concertina of walls. They layer centuries,
flourish a magic of window panes and solid,
panelled doors, arrange pewter plates as a chorus.
Inside, wine beads on goblet rims, children's footsteps echo
and, if I cease my incantations, in the pause I hear battle cries,
cannon fire, rips of lime mortar in the soil. My back to the river,
I summon carriage wheels on gravel, tapestries
of dropped stitches, book pages turning, whispered prayers.
Later, there are newspapers, Council letters on a silver tray,
the foreshadowing of road builders, the ceaseless rush of cars.
Others' spells were stronger though than mine,
there's no tarmac, Armco barrier, Catseyes – only archaeology,
the hush of fallen petals on a wooden floor.

Plunder

They must have arranged for someone to take
the leaded lights, parquet, Art Deco fireplace,
carpets, doors, lintels, tiles –
to leave the bricks and beams in a heap
like a giant's bring-and-buy.
And I, who had no rights, crept in at night,
a slipping-thief, soothed the *Danger* sign, *Keep Out!*,
goat-scrambled in the street-lamp dark,
unpicked from the rain what I could claim –
my mother's smile, my dancing feet,
walks with boys, hands in fallen leaves –
bound these things into a bone of wood
which used to be the attic stairs
and, weeping-thief, ran my plunder out.

Eleven Rooms

after Mondrian

I'm Alice, she says. Some days
I can reach the walls. Others
I'm a corner dot, so small the canvas

could swallow me whole if it wished.
In the vast red room, I'm taken, she says,
stretched stiff, fixed.

In the six greys (three dove,
three steel), I sometimes rest.
In the purple and yellow, I'm lost,

hazed, spaced. In the two black
I'm blind, can't measure
distance or time; *Temporary Girl*

they call me then. There are eleven rooms
in wonderland, she says.
No doors.

Ab Initio

And this is how it starts.
A room, a glance and after this a smile,

that search behind the eyes for lacework,
the stories which begin with this.

And we are cameras when we walk;
the river black, a whisper.

This London is theatre, its sky
footlit, and we talk in this bowl,

this hub of night, touch the touch that says
this is begun. And all that went before

is framed. And all we do is because of this:
this start, this room, this glance.

Dowry (i)

I bring with me my grandfather's apples –
brushed with newsprint, fingers
and heat – wrapped as though made from glass.

I bring with me the engine hum of wasps
and windfalls, quiet-cold earth;
his dugout, his shelter – its walls,

its cupped, dark air still heavy with war.
I bring with me the imprint of daisies,
lime-scented grass, his stooped back,

a Spitfire sun in his hair. I bring with me tang
and core and seed, the blush of skin, the silent season slip –
rain that beads and gathers like harvest.

Dowry (ii)

I give you the day my mother died, its winter slice –
lay it at your feet, ask you to shrine it.
There was the banded light, banding
through the call my father took, the seconds,

how they slowed and my hands and feet grew
vast – grew cosmic, immovable, how the walls
bred pinholes to galaxies where she still lived.
There was vague clamour as we strained to see

but they winked, these galaxies winked, they disappeared.
I give you the quiet days after to vacuum-wrap,
store in cupboards, in the corners of our house,
ask you to craft handles, tenderly close the door.

Marriage, Backwards

In the morning, rain shales the cottage window.
A bit like maracas,

an odd word for here, for Wales,
she thinks as they undress,

unmake the bed, sleep not touching
in the lean first light's retreat to midnight,

its dark awkwardness. She dreams
of music, notes that unstave and it's

evening, he unpours the wine, she tries
to talk about tomorrow, he tells

her about his day at work instead.
The Pinot Noir peels from her tongue,

leaves it smooth, colder than before,
the hour she waits for him, reads

Mrs Dalloway, pages ninety-nine
to sixty-five, hears his car unarrive,

looks at her watch to check the time.

Wall Angels

That morning, the last
of the holiday that winter
she'd wait for him to wake.

And through a gap in the curtains
the sun sent a saffron
aurora to dance on the wall.

The shadows of bare branches
were wings in the rhythm
of his sleep, and shapes like angels.

She'd mourn them
as they moved towards the door,
put out a hand to stop them

but, by the time he woke,
the sun had slipped a fraction,
they'd moved on.

Escapology

Last Sunday. The South Bank,
a low February sun, a camera obscura
of languages and the side shows:

Mr Marvel's Marvellous One-Way-Mirror Maze,
a laughing carousel (how I wanted
the horses to be real!), a human statue –

a Roundhead painted black, sitting
on a plinth, his coat a sheen. Next,
Larry the Lizard Man on a bicycle, and acrobats

holding one another high – tough men they were,
deft. At the skate park young bloods
swaggered, mimed careless flicks

of hair while their friends tagged
walls with aerosol cans. (A pretty girl
and a boy with a guitar sang

to an empty crowd.) Then the market
of books, rivers of them shining,
thin volumes of poems I leafed

through with my grandmother's hands.
You stood at a distance to take a photograph.
And, at the end,

under the bridge, near the hawker,
his cauldron of salted nuts a plangent echo
of something I could not quite place,

Ernesto the Escapologist snapped metal
rings around his arms, shiffled himself
into his sack and smiled his eyes at us.

Watch me get out of this, they seemed to say.

Fisherman

There is the waiting,
line pooled in a mercury of water,
finger poised to feel
the slightest shift of tension.

He senses the fish stir
deep where the reeds start,
sees her scales waver,
her subtle gleam of eye.

There is the flick of fin,
beat of tail and he answers,
Yes, you are mine.
Hook in lip, there is the drawing up,

both fish and man beguiled,
mesmerised for a while.
Then he lands her, eel-slim, smooth.
A moment's struggle follows

and he puts her by his foot,
looks at the patterns she makes,
at the flattening of grasses,
the crazy whisk of flesh.

He's ready now to free her,
honour her reclamation;
unfastens her to slither
back to the scent of water.

Soundless

                Imagine this
a roof top
the city shameless before you
edges of wind slicing your face

and windows
lit like rape
and her behind one
behind a laptop screen

looking up to smile
at someone you can't see
or perhaps she's cooking
searing meat

a drink by her side
her fingers slick
on wet glass
her phone rings

                Imagine a man
his hips on hers
their skin is shining
she will cry out

then sleep your name
wake to watch the dark retreat
as he breathes
the sheets white on him

                Imagine she has eyes
like cameras
is at a window
scanning the skyline

her heart soundless

Punctuation

We're making love and there's a comma on your shoulder.
It's shining in the dark –

part pause, part the start of separation.
Question marks are in your eyes.

I have no answer other than to press my lips
to your neck and feel you smile.

This moment's stolen, we're living in quotation marks.
Next you touch me with apostrophes –

silky on my skin, they brush my breasts with belonging.
I arch my back, our release is an exclamation.

Afterwards, the sheet's littered with semicolons,
colons, there are hyphens between our toes

and we speak ellipsis, promise each other
a lexicon without a word for grief, or any full stop –

Reversal

When I drive away, we'll each arrive
and I will see you touch my arm.
Time will make the sound of bees,

there'll be a dam of words
behind our teeth. Later, you'll kiss me
with a promise I already know we cannot keep

and I will see you touch my arm,
decide this is another way for us
to end, a way for us to start.

Talking to a Dead Horse

After the vet leaves, I craft
myself into the curl of your neck.

It's so quiet we can hear the spiders.
The stable floor's still warm,

it smells sweet, almost like honey
and in my head you're running,

are as eloquent as water,
have done this a thousand times

and I can tell you what he said
that first time, all the times after,

how his touch was amber,
that he likes Eggs Benedict for breakfast.

I can tell you what he doesn't know –
I can't stand geraniums or tapioca pudding,

The Sound of Music makes me cry,
there are thousands of unsaid words in my chest,

I miss him like mercury.
You listen and I love you.

Tomorrow they'll come and take you away.

Strada, Broad Street

Parmesan? The waiter asks. I nod.
He looks like he might weep.
I want to touch the cuff of his crisp white shirt
and tell him it's going to be OK,
I'm not going to say this used to be a flower shop
and once, after the first time, a boy like him
bought me lilies here, standing at the window
like a photograph, that he turned around
and smiled at me and we took the flowers home,
kissed each other hard on our mouths, in the hollows
of our arms, that years later, someone

did some tearing down, leaving the faint
curve of a wall, a row of trees, a space
filled with flats and furniture and cars of people
I've never met, and never will, that there's no proof.
The waiter moves away – slim hips, broad back.
He's glad I'm trapped at Table 2
with my wine for one, pasta and parmesan.
The lily scent still lingers. I find I'm crying now,
trying to trace a footprint I might have left behind
among the flower stems, and chairs, the promises I made.
He turns and smiles as someone new walks in.

The Love Song of Nowhere Place

The yellow smoke that slides along the street is
a condensation,
is characters from all books ever written –
mustard-quick,
a coagulant. And, after the novels, after
the teacups,
after the skirts that trail along the floor,
the women of
Nowhere Place will shiver home
to aspidistra leaves
and conversations in mahogany
until the dressing bell.
Then they'll fasten lovers' kisses
into bodices and stays,
button the thick touch of fingertips
into chiffon
and lace, remember the yellow
smoke, its quicksilver
breath, sit bone-straight, listen to husbands –
their afterward tales.

Afterwards

Afterwards, he suggests they walk.
She is, he thinks, diluted here.

The waitress fades, his cash
on her small silver tray and his tongue's

coated, thick with pizza, wine,
the word *beguiled*. He likes to walk,

for the crowds to part, for whichever
route they take to be a bid

to sidestep time, how her arm
will brush against his like static.

It's better than the want, the reach
across the table, the food she's hardly

touched, to put his hand on hers.
In the Burlington Arcade they stop awhile.

It's gaudy, she says, and nudges him,
the low hum in the back of her throat

astonishing, like the sound
she'd make afterwards, and afterwards

he remembers her vanish through
the entrance of the Tube,

be swallowed, how he waited, rooted,
for her to turn, smile.

Mistranslations

enlever – to take, remove
bien élevé – well raised

Summer '79: mattress heat, exams,
Thatcher, JPII's nine days, Ian Dury
and swarming air. Want: that buzz
beneath my breastbone, the thousand
things I don't yet know, and Room C3
with its windows wide-looking to the park,
its spill to Jubilee Road and leaves
the size of hands, green like dragon wings.

We wore navy, ties knotted into fists,
were defiant in mascara, skirts rolled at our waists.
Pens slipped between our fingers like fish
and that afternoon we translated French,
a passage about a girl, the trunk of a car
and one small word, *enlever*.
But in Room C3 I remembered Annecy,
its sideways light, chickens pocking

the yard, a low fence, Henri DuParc,
his barrel chest, folded eyes, the old, slow
burn of his smile. *He was in the Resistance*,
Dad had said and Madame's cotton dress
was listening; the soup came from Henri's
head, at least that was what I thought
he said. *Voilà, ma petite. Tu es bien élevé, non?*
His touch was warm, his breath was bread.

Dad laughed, *It was just the recipe
in his head.* So in Room c3 I bent the words
and told the story I wanted to tell,
now read your message on my phone,
think of the things you've taken –
your father's clock, your clothes,
the books, my damaged heart
and wonder could I mistranslate again.

Grattage

I start with the flesh on your neck.
The incision is soundless, my knife
bends at the first flake.

At this uncrease of skin I see layers
of tint, Jaune, glimpse the blank
beneath. Next I unpick

your hair, each strand unbristled,
unlit, that mix of Charcoal,
Raw Umber, Payne's Gray. Around

my feet the pieces fall and I sing
words of wreckage, my voice
is pigment, oil. Then it's where

you stand, the Lamp Black
and Pewter of it. This is my
undoing. My fingers bleed

the Doré of your lips, all
they didn't say, until I reach
the Burnt Sienna of your eyes,

and the end is that glint of white,
Cremnitz White, which was how
you chose to love me.

Cwm yr Adar

for Elaine

When I was a child the valley's voice
was an old man's voice.
It sang of hush and earth.

It wove the fields to the hem of the sea,
lifted gulls on its wings, bent
the weather back. From our bright

white house on the hill I listened
to it curve, tracked it in elderflower,
vetch, watched it flutter like litter

on the sands, between the tea-shop chairs.
After school I ran it high on the cliff, ran it young.
It snapped like a kite's dip, a kite's crackle.

And now is harder than I thought.
The valley's voice is a bricked-up voice,
full of mutter and clamour and snag.

Outside the new Lifeguard hut
my beach-born breath's held by a salt wind,
by the force of a hundred hands.

Llantwit Sands

She's on the sands again,
in the grey, drawn, too early day.
I watch the cliffs' shadow, sea
swell small laceworks as she walks.

It's like this more often now, days
grey, drawn, too early really,
she and I both mapping
footprints which aren't there.

When she's gone I cannot see her
in rooms, furnitured, mirrored
above the fire. She's always here
on the sands and I am watching her.

When she's gone, I cannot see her
in rooms, furnitured, mirrored
above the fire. She's always here

on the sands and I am watching her
in the grey, drawn, too early day,
with the cliffs shadowing, sea

swelling to small laceworks as she walks.
It's like this more often now, the two of us
mapping footprints in the grey, drawn day. Too early really.

Malta

for Jez

Leaving Mdina we didn't speak.
All that could be said had soaked

its high walls, its soft stone, been cast
wide across laced plains to the sea.

We'd dined, the sky caught by orange trees,
rosemary, marjoram, mint.

We'd whispered small prayers
to the shadows of a hundred

doorway cats and, in the cathedral-quiet
the sun had hummed, had strummed.

And we came here to the hallelujah
of Sliema's evening streets,

the snackle of roof-top washing,
bell-peal of Our Lady Star of the Sea,

and this fiesta: this bud and bloom
of fireworks, dance –

the beat between each flare
and roar as long as silence, love.

Cuffs

for Nan

In the crackling heat my grandmother
is hanging out the wash,
watched by his marigolds, the privet, me,

is held small in this vertical air,
safe in the absence of war. She's deft,
seamless with his shirts, their snackle,

blind of white, grips a cuff,
brings it to her lips, smiles her turquoise eyes
at something he must once have said.

Exhibition

In the white room the walls are patient. The woodblock floor has, deep down, some remnant of cigarette smoke and how she imagines the Thirties to have been. A van stops on double-yellows outside the door, men carry her pictures in and she remembers her mother telling her once that it's unlucky to tread on butterflies. She holds her breath as she tries to think if she ever has, wishes she hadn't had the coffee that's swilling in her throat, tasting somehow brackish. Her pictures rest against the skirting, the order of them like poetry perhaps, how she's heard books of them should bear scrutiny, have some inbuilt synchronicity, let the reader see the inner workings of the heart. She watches men hang her art in the patient room with its white walls and waits for the public to come, curious to read the story she's written them, see the cracks and flaws she's painted over, painted in.

Photograph, 1959

My mother's hands are at rest
on the tabletop. She is
a still life of cigarette smoke and satin,
is smiling, has eleven years to go.

To her right my father's
hopeful head bends to listen. He is
slender, cradles me as a spark
somewhere between his pocket and his eye.

My hands hold the photograph,
are the hands my mother's
would have been had they grown old.
They conjure on keyboards

and in kitchens, rarely rest,
knit chronicles with veins
and scars. They are her testament,
her album, her frame.

Taking Tea at the Savoy

We're taking tea at the Savoy
and all is how it should be.

The cups are Wedgwood shells,
waiters flit in circles like birds,

the air is lifted, music.
There's people-hum,

cakes that taste of lavender cream;
the floor is lush, the walls are gold,

roses blush in silver bowls.
The dome is glass, is gold and evening,

the sun setting in marmalade flares
and all is how it should be.

She's fifty, I am forty-eight
and the sugar tongs

are weighty as we talk.
Our table's laid for four

and in the empty chairs
she's eleven, I'm nine.

We smile, are wise.
They have no idea who we are.

It Sparks

It is tiny and it sparks,
murmurs me into believing that sunlight
will make cathedrals in the bracken,
there will be cheese on toast after Sauvignon Blanc,
grey-green skies and Wimbledon,
the weight of you in me, skin-to-skin,
my sons will be the men they should become,
sheets will applaud as they dry on the line,
always the sideways dance of crabs,
an unfolded September morning,
books, music, laughter, rain,
long, long shadows in the dusk,
the *News at Ten*, lavender, heat.
It is tiny, and it sparks.

Cader Idris

for Dad

That day we climbed Cader
the air was vinegar hot.
Walking the scree was wading,
eyes hurt from its rattle and grab.

Craig Cau was a slab of kingfisher
water to dive to, slice through,
but you had hold of my hand.
Pen y Gadair was curve and ocean,

our huge high sun within reach
and later, the evening was purple,
the men of Dolgellau made fire in the valley,
sang seamless to me, moon and mountain,

to the heat of the horses, the willow-strong
farmer's boy. Next day was leaving.
All now is contours.
The map's in a drawer back at home.

Afterword: Dearest

I'm sitting by the window.
The sea's knocking on the lamp
and the nib of my pen, is asking to come in.
I'm writing – *Dearest, it's galling, but*
(and the sea knows this already)
there's a gull banking on the wind
as grasses shift to the shore,
its wings scratch a W on the clouds
and I still love you, wonder if it's too late
to say I'm by the window, the sea asking
to come in, trying to stop me from saying
if you could come back, would you?
PS, the gull's gone.
And so now has the sea.

Two Rivers Press has been publishing in and about Reading since 1994. Founded by the artist Peter Hay (1951–2003), the press continues to delight readers, local and further afield, with its varied list of individually designed, thought-provoking books.